Discover Planets

Discover

Saturn

Georgia Beth

Lerner Publications ◆ Minneapolis

Lerner Publications Company
A division of Lerner Publishing Group, Inc.
241 First Avenue North
Minneapolis, MN 55401 USA

For reading levels and more information, look up this title
at www.lernerbooks.com.

Main body text set in Adrianna Regular 14/20.
Typeface provided by Chank.

Library of Congress Cataloging-in-Publication Data

Names: Beth, Georgia, author.
Title: Discover Saturn / Georgia Beth.
Description: Minneapolis : Lerner Publications, [2018] | Series: Searchlight books.
   Discover planets | Audience: Ages 8–11. | Audience: Grades 4 to 6. | Includes
   bibliographical references and index.
Identifiers: LCCN 2017061819 (print) | LCCN 2017056671 (ebook) |
   ISBN 9781541525467 (eb pdf) | ISBN 9781541523395 (lb : alk. paper) |
   ISBN 9781541527898 (pb : alk. paper)
Subjects: LCSH: Saturn (Planet)—Exploration—Juvenile literature. | Saturn (Planet)—
   Juvenile literature.
Classification: LCC QB671 (print) | LCC QB671 .B48 2018 (ebook) | DDC 523.46—dc23

LC record available at https://lccn.loc.gov/2017061819

Manufactured in the United States of America
1-44412-34671-2/7/2018

Contents

Chapter 1

BRIGHT AND BEAUTIFUL

Saturn has inspired skygazers for hundreds of years. Many consider this large planet to be the most beautiful in the solar system. With the naked eye, Saturn looks like a bright light in the sky. But through a telescope, you can see Saturn's swirling atmosphere and thousands of rings.

The white arrow in this image points at Saturn. It's visible below Venus, the brightest planet in the night sky.

SATURN IS KNOWN FOR ITS RINGS. THEY ARE BOLD AND EASY TO SEE.

Saturn is the second-largest planet in our solar system. It is about 227,348 miles (365,882 km) around. That's about nine times bigger than Earth. But Saturn is also the least dense planet. That means the gas and rock that make up Saturn is not packed together as tightly as it is on other planets.

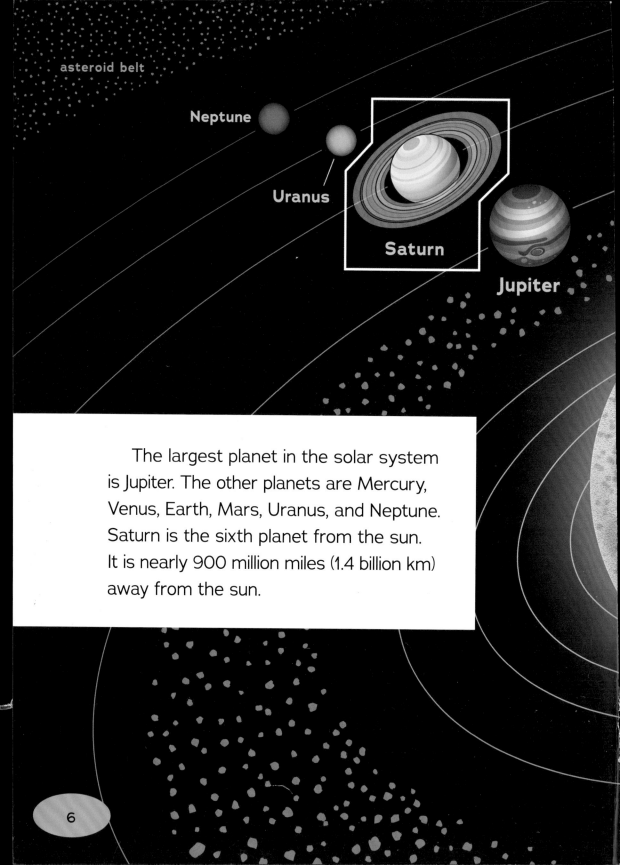

asteroid belt

Neptune

Uranus

Saturn

Jupiter

The largest planet in the solar system
is Jupiter. The other planets are Mercury,
Venus, Earth, Mars, Uranus, and Neptune.
Saturn is the sixth planet from the sun.
It is nearly 900 million miles (1.4 billion km)
away from the sun.

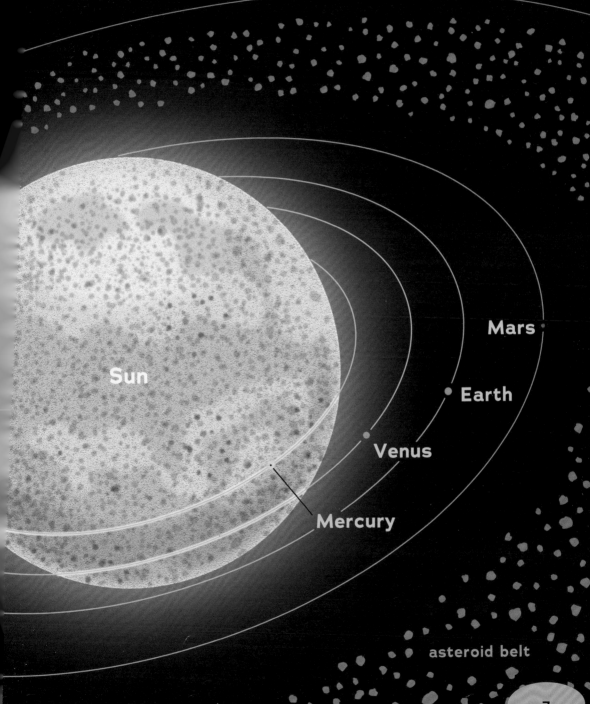

The Solar System

Sun

Mercury

Venus

Earth

Mars

asteroid belt

Spinning in Space

All the planets orbit the sun. Earth takes about 365 days, or one year, to orbit the sun. Saturn's orbit takes much longer. Saturn takes twenty-nine Earth years to travel around the sun once. The orbit is 886,489,415 miles (1,426,666,422 km) long. As the planets travel around the sun, they also spin. The time it takes a planet to spin around once is 1 day. A day on Earth is 24 hours. On Saturn, a day is just 10.5 hours.

As planets orbit the sun, one side of the planet faces the sun and is bright while the other side is dark.

STEM Highlight

What do you get when you rapidly spin a planet that's not very dense? A squishy planet! Saturn rotates so quickly that it is 7,500 miles (12,070 km) wider at the center than it is at the poles. That's 10 percent wider than it is tall! This shape is an oblate spheroid. Jupiter, Uranus, and Neptune are also oblate spheroids, but the shape is most visible on Saturn. Astronomers can easily see its squished shape through a telescope.

The thick middle part of an oblate spheroid is known as the equatorial bulge.

Chapter 2

A STRANGE PLACE

On Earth, it is easy to feel the ground under our feet. But Saturn isn't solid like Earth. Instead, it is made up of gases such as helium and hydrogen. A thick layer of clouds surrounds the planet. Underneath the gas and clouds, Saturn has a layer of liquid hydrogen. Then there is a layer of liquid metallic hydrogen. Saturn's center is a core made up of rock and ice.

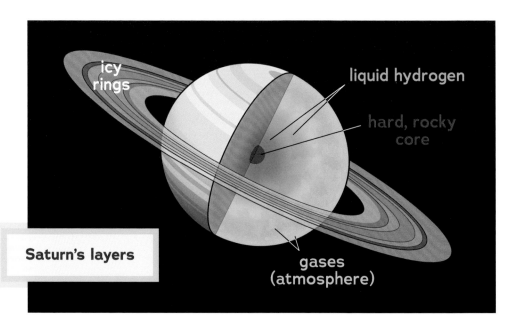

icy rings

liquid hydrogen

hard, rocky core

Saturn's layers

gases (atmosphere)

Saturn's atmosphere is cold and stormy. At its north pole, there is a six-sided spinning vortex of air. The winds in the storm can reach 310 miles (500 km) per hour. The area is 20,000 miles (32,190 km) wide. Smaller storms are inside the larger storm. One is 1,243 miles (2,000 km) wide.

The spacecraft *Cassini* took this photo of the stormy vortex at Saturn's north pole. Color was added to the image to make the storms and clouds appear more vivid.

STEM Highlight

Just like Earth, Saturn has different seasons. Both Earth and Saturn tilt slightly, so as they move around the sun, half of the planet is closer to the sun than the other half. On Earth, it is summer in the part of the planet tilted toward the sun and winter in the part tilted away from the sun. Saturn's seasons last much longer than Earth's do. Because Saturn takes so long to orbit the sun, each season can be more than seven years long.

The Hubble Space Telescope took these images of Saturn from 1996 to 2000 as the planet's northern half tilted away from the sun.

Moons and Rings

Many pieces of ice and rock orbit Saturn. These pieces can be as large as a mountain or as small as a snowflake. The largest objects orbiting Saturn are moons. Saturn has about sixty known moons. Only Jupiter has more moons.

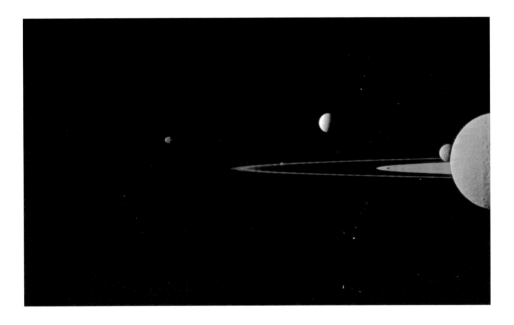

FIVE OF SATURN'S MOONS ARE VISIBLE IN THIS IMAGE.

Titan is Saturn's largest moon. It is larger than Mercury. Titan has a thick atmosphere. Toxic chemicals rain from the sky on Titan. Some other moons have unique characteristics too. Enceladus appears to have ice volcanoes and intense streams of water spewing from it. Scientists think that moons are constantly being created and destroyed around Saturn as pieces of ice and rock collide.

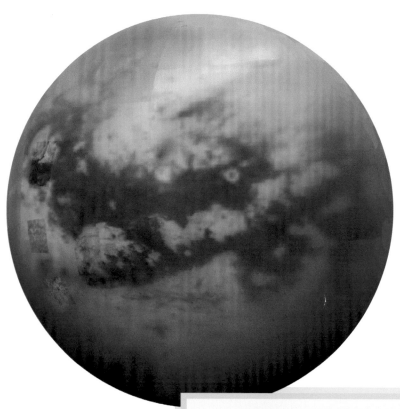

An infrared instrument on *Cassini* took this image of Titan.

This image, taken by *Cassini* in 2009, clearly shows Saturn's rings.

From far away, the ice and rock around Saturn appears grouped into seven rings. Each ring is very large but very thin. Scientists think the rings formed when a comet or asteroid hit an icy moon and broke it into pieces.

Scientists refer to each of the rings by a different letter of the alphabet. The biggest rings are A, B, and C. They were discovered first. Later, smaller and fainter rings were found. The D ring is closest to Saturn. The E ring is farthest away.

Chapter 3

LONG LOOKS AND FAST FLYBYS

Saturn has fascinated people for hundreds of years. In 1610, Italian astronomer Galileo Galilei discovered Saturn. He was able to see the planet and its rings through a telescope. But he thought he was seeing a planet and two moons that were too close to each other to tell them apart. Later, the Dutch astronomer Christiaan Huygens used a stronger telescope. He saw that Saturn was one planet with rings. Huygens also saw Titan.

This illustration shows Galileo peering through a telescope around 1620.

The First Flyby

In the twentieth century, scientists began sending spacecraft to explore the solar system. They wanted to see the planets up close. In 1979, *Pioneer 11* flew past Saturn. *Pioneer 11* carried telescopes, cameras, and scientific instruments to measure light and temperature. The spacecraft took pictures and measurements of Saturn.

An artist's image shows *Pioneer 11* approaching Saturn.

Pioneer 11 took this image of Saturn and Titan. The spacecraft was 1,768,422 miles (2,846,000 km) from the planet.

From *Pioneer 11*, scientists learned that Saturn is mostly made of liquid hydrogen. The spacecraft's instruments recorded temperatures of -292°F (-180°C). *Pioneer 11* also found the moon Epimetheus and Saturn's F ring.

Voyager Mission

In the 1980s, *Voyager 1* and *Voyager 2* flew by Saturn. Scientists wanted to get closer to Saturn and learn more about its rings and moons. Instruments on *Voyager 1* measured the hydrogen and helium in Saturn's atmosphere. *Voyager 1* also found three new moons and Saturn's G ring.

Voyager 2 took this image of Saturn's B ring in August 1981.

Voyager 1 and *Voyager 2* were designed to complete a five-year mission to Jupiter and Saturn. The spacecraft were so successful that the mission was extended. *Voyager 1* flew deep into space, while *Voyager 2* went on to fly by Uranus and Neptune. *Voyager 2* was able to visit all four planets because these planets were arranged in a way that happens only about once every 175 years. The spacecraft could move from planet to planet using each planet's gravity and orbit rather than using extra energy and fuel. This strategy is known as gravity assist.

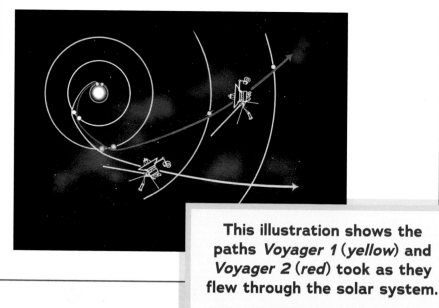

This illustration shows the paths *Voyager 1* (*yellow*) and *Voyager 2* (*red*) took as they flew through the solar system.

Voyager 1 and Voyager 2 flew through the solar system and sent back data to Earth for more than forty years. Then they left the solar system and began exploring distant areas of space. Scientists hope the spacecraft will continue sending information from space until they eventually lose power, around 2025.

ONE OF THE VOYAGER SPACECRAFT TOOK THIS DISTANT IMAGE OF JUPITER'S PLACE IN THE SOLAR SYSTEM.

Chapter 4

A CLOSER LOOK

In 1997, NASA launched the *Cassini* spacecraft to study Saturn and its moons in more detail. *Cassini* flew between Saturn's rings and sent back photographs for thirteen years. The mission was designed to last just five years. But *Cassini*'s team made sure *Cassini* had backup instruments and extra fuel if anything went wrong on the mission. When *Cassini* completed its mission, it still worked for eight more years.

An artist's image shows *Cassini* flying between Saturn and its rings.

Looking for Life

Cassini carried the *Huygens* probe to Titan. In 2005, *Huygens* landed there. It sent back images of large hills of sand created by the wind. Volcanoes that explode with water instead of lava may be there. And a sea of water may be underground. Nearby Enceladus sends oxygen to Titan. Scientists have found other organic molecules on Titan too. Scientists believe that with these ingredients, life might be able to survive on Titan.

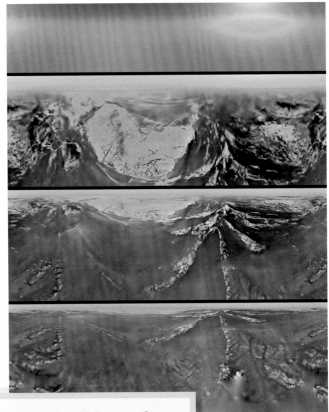

Huygens took these images of the surface of Titan from four different heights.

The atmosphere of Titan is so thick that we cannot see Titan's surface through telescope images. The *Huygens* probe gave us our first look at Titan. The probe had a hard shell to protect it from burning up as it moved through Titan's atmosphere. Equipment inside the shell controlled *Huygens* after it separated from *Cassini*. Several scientific instruments gathered information about Titan's atmosphere and surface. *Huygens* moved through Titan's atmosphere in two hours and twenty-seven minutes.

An artist's image based on photos taken by *Huygens* shows the probe on the surface of Titan.

Enceladus also may have life. *Cassini* took images of water shooting from the ground. The spacecraft flew through the water and detected organic molecules. Scientists want to learn more about Enceladus and the molecules there.

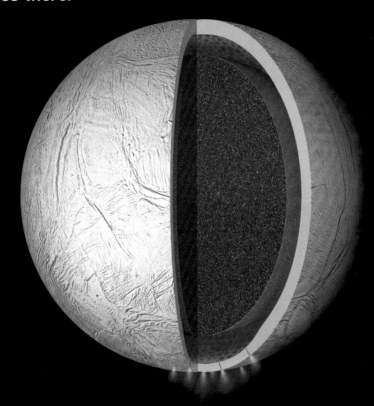

This illustration shows what the inside of Enceladus may look like.

The Grand Finale

At the end of *Cassini*'s journey, there wasn't enough fuel to visit another moon or go farther into space. *Cassini* spent its last months flying between Saturn and its rings. With ice and rocks in every direction, it was risky. But *Cassini* was able to study Saturn's cloud tops and look for clues about how the rings formed. *Cassini* mapped the inner layers of the planet too.

This image of the northern part of Saturn is one of the last images *Cassini* sent back to Earth in 2017.

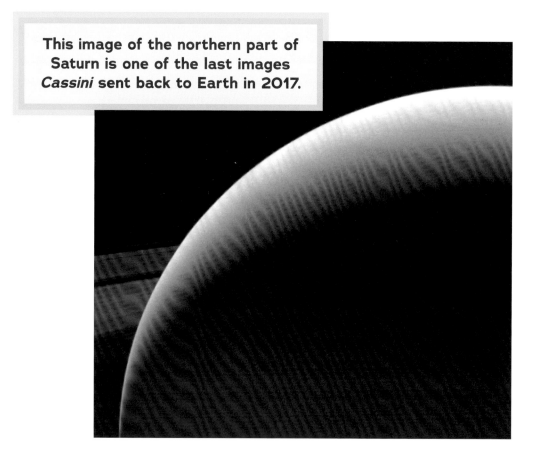

An illustration shows *Cassini* as it moves through Saturn's atmosphere.

In 2017, *Cassini*'s mission officially ended. Scientists sent the spacecraft into Saturn's atmosphere to burn up. That way it wouldn't crash into something else or contaminate one of Saturn's moons.

Scientists will study the data from *Cassini* for years. They hope to send another spacecraft to Saturn to make even more discoveries. Scientists want to know more about Saturn's atmosphere. They want to explore the depths of Titan's seas and fly over Enceladus. Scientists are excited to find out if any of Saturn's moons have ever had life.

Taken by *Cassini* in September 2017, this image shows the moon Enceladus beyond the edge of Saturn.

Looking Ahead

- Saturn's rings appear to rain into the atmosphere. This rain creates dark bands of clouds and affects the temperature of Saturn's atmosphere.

- *Cassini* sent back an image of a small icy object on the edge of Saturn's A ring. It may be a new moon. Scientists will need to study more images to know for sure. Until then, they are calling the object Peggy.

- When the next mission to Saturn occurs, scientists likely will be looking for signs of life.

Glossary

atmosphere: the gases that surround a planet

data: information

gravity: a force that pulls objects in space toward one another

moon: a large, round object that orbits a planet

orbit: to travel around another object in an oval or circular path

organic molecule: a small particle found in living things

probe: a device used to travel to and send back information from outer space

solar system: the group of planets and other objects in space that orbit the sun

toxic: poisonous

vortex: spinning liquid or air with an area in the center that pulls things in

Learn More about Saturn

Books

Goldstein, Margaret J. *Discover Jupiter.* Minneapolis: Lerner Publications, 2019. Find out about another large planet explored in the Pioneer and Voyager missions.

Hamilton, John. *Cassini: Unlocking the Secrets of Saturn.* Minneapolis: Abdo, 2018. Learn more about the Cassini mission to Saturn, including information about *Cassini*'s construction, launch, and discoveries.

Squire, Ann. *Planet Saturn.* New York: Children's Press, 2014. Read more about what Saturn is made of, its orbit, and its history.

Websites

ESA Kids
https://www.esa.int/esaKIDSen/SEMJL6WJD1E_OurUniverse_0.html
Find information about Saturn, its moons and rings, and the Cassini mission.

NASA Solar System Exploration
https://solarsystem.nasa.gov/kids/do-it-yourself/
Discover activities and information about Saturn and its place in the solar system.

PBS Kids Ready Jet Go!
http://pbskids.org/learn/readyjetgo/
Join the Ready Jet Go crew as they fly through Saturn's rings, play a solar system game, and learn more about all the planets in the solar system.

Index

Photo Acknowledgments

The images in this book are used with the permission of: Jamie Cooper/SSPL/Getty Images, pp. 4; NASA/JPL-Caltech/Space Science Institute, pp. 5, 8, 11, 13, 26, 28; Laura Westlund/Independent Picture Service, pp. 6–7, 10; NASA/JPL/SSI, pp. 9, 15; R. G. French (Wellesley College) et al., NASA, ESA, and The Hubble Heritage Team (STScI/AURA), p. 12; NASA/JPL/University of Arizona/University of Idaho, p. 14; Hulton Archive/Getty Images, p. 16; NASA Ames, pp. 17, 18; NASA/JPL, p. 19; Sally Bensusen/Science Source, p. 20; Time Life Pictures/JPL/NASA/The LIFE Picture Collection/Getty Images, p. 21; NASA, p. 22; ESA/NASA/JPL/University of Arizona, p. 23; ESA, p. 24; NASA/JPL-Caltech, pp. 25, 27.

Cover: NASA/JPL-Caltech/SSI.